MW01134381

All the material in this book was confirmed as accurate at the time of publication.

The names, trademarks, and logos of the named entities and brands profiled in this book are the property of their respective owners and are used solely for identification purposes. This book is a publication of Quarto Publishing plc and it has not been prepared, approved, endorsed, or licensed by any other brand, person, or entity.

For my mom and dad, who introduced me to so many amazing places.—N.D.

To my beloved Sister and Brother-in-law Amy and Stephen Graham.—J.M-P.

Text © 2025 Nancy Dickmann. Illustrations © 2025 J. Moffat-Peña

First published in 2025 by Wide Eyed Editions, an imprint of The Quarto Group.
100 Cummings Center, Suite 265D, Beverly, MA 01915, USA.
T +1 978-282-9590 www.Quarto.com
EEA Representation, WTS Tax d.o.o., Žanova ulica 3, 4000 Kranj, Slovenia.

The right of Nancy Dickmann to be identified as the author and J. Moffat-Peña to be identified as the illustrator of this work has been asserted by them in accordance with the Copyright, Designs and Patents Act, 1988 (United Kingdom).

All rights reserved.

No part of this publication may be reproduced, stored in a retrieval system, or transmitted, in any form, or by any means, electrical, mechanical, photocopying, recording, or otherwise without the prior written permission of the publisher or a license permitting restricted copying.

ISBN 978-1-8360-0129-4
eBook ISBN 978-1-8360-0130-0

The illustrations were created digitally
Set in Quicksand and Thirsty Script

Designer: Victoria Vassiades
Editor: Leah Baxter
Production Controller: Dawn Cameron
Art Director: Karissa Santos
Publisher: Debbie Foy

Manufactured in Guangdong, China TT022025

9 8 7 6 5 4 3 2 1

FSC
www.fsc.org
MIX
Paper | Supporting
responsible forestry
FSC® C016973

Only in
THE PACIFIC
NORTHWEST

Written by **Nancy Dickmann** · Illustrated by **J. Moffat–Peña**

WIDE EYED EDITIONS

Contents

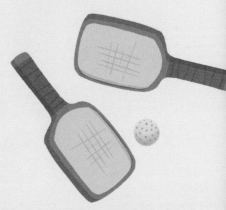

Welcome to the Pacific Northwest

Everyone has a different idea of a dream vacation. Some people go for jaw-dropping scenery with mountains, lakes, rugged coastlines, and lush forests. Others prefer the excitement of cities full of quirky restaurants and live performances. But whatever it is that you're looking for, you're likely to find it in the Pacific Northwest! Often known as Cascadia or the PNW, this region is famous for its natural beauty and hip music and food scenes, as well as a progressive culture all about tolerance and living in harmony with the natural environment. Let's take a tour of this fascinating region, exploring all the weird and wonderful landscapes, people, festivals, and attractions that make the PNW unique!

N
E
W
S

Turn on that light! Winter in the PNW is known as the BIG DARK. It's so far north that some days have less than 8 hours of daylight.

The 49TH PARALLEL cuts through the PNW. Since 1846, it has formed the border between the western parts of Canada and the United States.

BRITISH COLUMBIA

CANADA

JUNEAU

ALASKA

A land without borders

Where exactly is the Pacific Northwest? Well, it depends on who you ask! Most people would say it includes the northern lands between the Pacific Ocean and the Rocky Mountains. The Cascade Mountains form the region's spine, running north to south. But how far north, and how far south? The most common definitions include Washington, Oregon, and British Columbia in Canada. Many include northern Idaho, and some even pull in parts of northern California and southern Alaska. The different definitions look for similarities in the land, wildlife, and culture. To the people that live there, the PNW is more than just a region marked on a map. It's a state of mind!

Stay on your toes! The Cascades are home to several ACTIVE VOLCANOES, including Mount St. Helens.

The Pacific Northwest is famous for its LUSH FORESTS, fed by plenty of rain.

VANCOUVER

WASHINGTON

SEATTLE

IDAHO

PORTLAND

OREGON

Portland Oregon

OLD TOWN

UNITED STATES OF AMERICA

CALIFORNIA

Built for the 1962 World's Fair, the SPACE NEEDLE provides amazing views over the city. You can climb the 848 steps to the top, or just zoom up on the elevator.

The Space Needle is linked to other attractions by a space-age MONORAIL that weaves between the skyscrapers.

At the historic PIKE PLACE MARKET shoppers can see a giant bronze piggy bank called Rachel and watch fish-sellers playing catch with salmon before stopping for a drink at the original Starbucks coffee shop.

The well-loved THREE GIRLS BAKERY, established in 1912, was the first business in Seattle where the business license was issued to women.

Where can you see a two-story "tornado" made of guitars, alongside props and costumes from sci-fi and horror films? At the MUSEUM OF POP CULTURE, of course!

Outside Seattle's famous ART MUSEUM, a moving 48-foot statue shows a man hammering over . . . and over . . . and over. But on Labor Day, this hard-working statue gets the day off!

Local artist Dale Chihuly is a glass-blowing pioneer, and CHIHULY GARDEN AND GLASS showcases some of his most amazing work.

Seattle

We'll start our tour in the region's biggest metro area. Located on the shores of Puget Sound, Seattle is a city that has it all—from waterfront beauty to towering skyscrapers, historic buildings and museums, hip cafés and stores, and a thriving music scene. Seattle has a well-deserved reputation for being quirky and cool, drawing people from all over the country.

Everyone knows that trolls lurk under bridges, and Seattle has its very own troll! The huge FREMONT TROLL statue looks as though the creature is crawling out of the earth to crush a car.

The tech giant Amazon had its start in Seattle, and the company's headquarters are still found in the city. Workers, and sometimes local residents, have an incredible perk—access to three amazing GLASS SPHERES that contain fish tanks, waterfalls, and an indoor rainforest.

At the SEATTLE AQUARIUM you'll come face-to-face with local sea creatures such as sharks, sea otters, and giant clams.

On a clear day, from the right vantage point you can see the snowy peak of MOUNT RAINIER towering in the distance.

Seattle's historic WATERFRONT is the place to go to see ferries, fireboats, and cruise ships.

Ever since 1906 trains have stopped at KING STREET STATION, which has a clock tower inspired by the famous bell tower in Venice, Italy.

Stats & Facts

FAST FACTS

ABBREVIATION: PNW
ALTERNATIVE NAME: Cascadia
LARGEST METRO AREA: Seattle (population of about 4 million people)
NUMBER OF COUNTRIES: 2 (USA and Canada)

A few people in the PNW still speak CHINOOK JARGON, a simplified language once used by fur traders. It was based on the language of the indigenous Chinook people, mixed with a smattering of French and English.

Driving along the Cariboo Highway in British Columbia, you'll see the world's largest CROSS-COUNTRY SKIS, measuring 40 feet high. Even the ski poles are a whopping 30 feet long!

WHAT'S ON THE LIST?

The PNW doesn't have defined borders, so it's impossible to give specific figures for things like population or land area. This also means that some of the superlatives are hard to pin down. For example, many people might say that Mount Rainier in Washington is the region's highest peak. And at 14,410 feet, it's certainly tall! But there are other mountains farther north that are taller, such as Mount Logan in Yukon and Mount Saint Elias on the Alaska/Yukon border. Would they make your list?

Based on their sustainable transportation and renewable energy use, Portland and Seattle regularly appear near the tops of lists ranking the GREENEST CITIES in the United States.

Next-Door Neighbors

NORTH: Alaska, Yukon   WEST: Pacif

FLYING THE DOUG

Many people in the PNW region proudly fly a flag known as "the Doug."
Designed in 1994 by Alexander Baretich, the flag's blue stripe represents
the sky and the region's many waterways, while the white stands for snow
and clouds and the green represents forests and fields. At the center is a
black silhouette of one of the region's famous Douglas fir trees.

REGIONAL RECORDS:

• In 1932, the Waterton-Glacier International Peace Park
was set up, becoming the world's first INTERNATIONAL PARK.
It covers land in both the United States and Canada.
• In 2019, Portland set a Guinness World Record for the
largest BLANKET FORT, measuring 6,736 square feet.
• Portland has won the crown as the most VEGAN-FRIENDLY CITY.
• The PNW generally has a cool climate, but in 2023 temperatures in Eugene,
Oregon hit 105°F, while in 2021 Lytton in British Columbia reached a SIZZLING 121°F!
• Washington is home to the USA'S LONGEST BEACH, stretching for about 28 miles.
But on the list of beaches with the most creative names, Long Beach must come last.
• British Columbia's Whistler ski area is home to the world'd longest SINGLE-SPAN CABLE CAR,
which travels 2.7 miles from one mountain peak to another. Just don't look down!

Ocean   SOUTH: California, Nevada   EAST: Idaho, Montana, Alberta

Portland

As cities go, Portland is truly unique. Its unofficial motto has long been "Keep Portland Weird," and the artists, chefs, musicians, and entrepreneurs that have flocked there over the years have done their best to keep this promise! Its funky vibe and reputation for being progressive, tolerant, and eco-friendly set it apart. Oregon's largest city straddles the banks of the Willamette River and sits just south of the Columbia River, which forms the border between Oregon and Washington.

Follow your nose to the International Rose Test Garden, where hundreds of varieties of roses have been grown for more than a century. Portland's climate is perfect for growing these fragrant blooms, leading to its nickname "CITY OF ROSES."

Some of Portland's sidewalks still have the IRON HORSE RINGS that were once used to tether horses, back when they outnumbered cars and bikes. Today, people have tethered little toy horses to many of them!

Portland is famous for its FOOD CARTS AND FOOD TRUCKS, selling everything from fried egg sandwiches to Korean tacos and hand-pulled noodles. Some carts are permanently parked in groups called "pods."

The PORTLAND AERIAL TRAM, nicknamed "the pill on the hill," connects the South Waterfront area with the hilltop campus of the Oregon Health and Science University.

One of Portland's most beautiful parks is built on top of an extinct volcano! The paths in MOUNT TABOR PARK are paved with pieces of ancient lava, and every year it hosts a soapbox derby race.

Portland's SATURDAY MARKET is the largest arts and crafts fair in the United States. Live bands play and you can buy local foods and crafts. Everything on sale must be made by hand!

You've probably heard of getting lost in a good book, but you can truly get lost at Powell's City of Books. It takes up an entire city block and stocks over 1 million books, making it the world's LARGEST BOOKSTORE!

California may be home to Silicon Valley, but Portland has its own area of high-tech firms, known as the SILICON FOREST.

At about six times the size of New York's Central Park, FOREST PARK has more than 70 miles of trails for joggers, bikers, and hikers, as well as a creepy old ruin known as the "Witch's Castle."

Known as a "living museum of trees," HOYT ARBORETUM contains over 2,000 different species of trees and shrubs, with trees originating from every continent except Antarctica. Many of them are now rare or endangered.

History Timeline

1.5 million–12,000 years ago The Columbian mammoth roamed the southern parts of the PNW. This extinct mammal is now Washington's official state fossil!

About 10,000–5,000 years ago Indigenous groups such as the Haida, Chinook, and Coast Salish first began living on the PNW coastline, going on to settle in permanent villages along the region's rivers and on its islands.

1579 The English privateer Sir Francis Drake lands somewhere along the northern Pacific coast, likely in what is now Oregon or northern California.

1846 The United States and the United Kingdom sign the Oregon Treaty to establish the border between the U.S. and Canada, along the 49th parallel. Indigenous peoples were not consulted about the border.

1845 The name of the new city of Portland is decided by a coin toss. If the penny had landed the other way up, the city would be called Boston!

1848 The U.S. government sets up the Oregon Territory, which included all of present-day Oregon and Washington, as well as parts of Idaho, Montana, and Wyoming.

1854 Chief Si'ahl of the Duwamish and Suquamish people gives a speech in response to a proposal from the U.S. government to buy their land, saying "this land is sacred to us."

1859 Oregon becomes the 33rd state admitted to the Union.

1861–1865 During the American Civil War, both the state of Oregon and Washington Territory fight on the side of the Union.

1977 Dixy Lee Ray becomes the first female governor of Washington.

1977 The Seattle Mariners baseball team joins the major leagues.

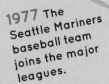

1962 Seattle hosts the World's Fair. The towering Space Needle and a monorail were built for the fair.

1955 Washington doctor Karl William Edmark invents the portable heart defibrillator.

1980 Washington volcano Mount Saint Helens erupts, sending out clouds of ash and blasting off part of the mountain's north slope.

1985 Bud Clark is elected mayor of Portland and works to improve public transportation and end housing insecurity.

1991 The band Nirvana, from Washington, releases the album *Nevermind*, helping make the local grunge music style widely popular.

2001 Iona Victoria Campagnolo becomes the first woman to serve as Lieutenant Governor of British Columbia.

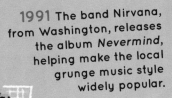

1700 A huge earthquake shakes the region, causing a tsunami that hits the coast of Japan.

1760s–1860s Traders from Russia, Britain, and the United States sail along the coast, trading with the Indigenous peoples for furs, mainly from sea otters.

1776 The United States Declaration of Independence is signed.

1778 Captain James Cook explores the coast, landing at Nootka Sound on Vancouver Island and trading for sea otter furs with the local Mowachaht people.

1793 The Scottish explorer Alexander Mackenzie becomes the first known traveler to cross Canada on land, reaching the Pacific Ocean at Bella Coola, British Columbia.

1844 George Washington Bush leads a group of settlers along the Oregon Trail but is barred from settling in Oregon because he is Black. He and his group continue north, across the Columbia River, and set up the first permanent American settlement in the area around Puget Sound.

1840s Settlers from the eastern and central United States begin to travel west by covered wagon along the Oregon Trail. They often settled on land that had been taken from Indigenous peoples.

1805 With the assistance of numerous Indigenous individuals and groups, as well as an enslaved person named York (who was a skilled navigator and explorer), the team led by Meriwether Lewis and William Clark reaches the Pacific Ocean by land, making their group the first U.S. expedition to do so.

1871 The Canadian province of British Columbia is established.

1872–1873 The U.S. government fights a war against the Modoc people in northern California and southern Oregon.

1877 Chief Heinmot Tooyalakekt (also known Chief Joseph) leads 300 Nimiipuu (Nez Perce) warriors in a fight against 2,000 U.S. soldiers as a result of the U.S. breaking their agreed land treaty. He is forced to surrender, declaring "I will fight no more forever."

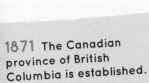

1889 Washington becomes the 42nd state admitted to the Union.

1942 The Grand Coulee Dam opens on the Columbia River in Washington, providing hydroelectric power to a wide area.

1940 The Tacoma Narrows Bridge, crossing part of Puget Sound, is opened. It collapses later that year.

1899 President William McKinley establishes Mount Rainier National Park. Crater Lake National Park, Kootenay National Park in Canada and Olympic National Park all follow in the next 21 years.

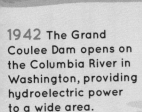

2005 The Oregon children's author Beverly Cleary, who wrote the *Ramona Quimby* books, is honored as a "living legend" by the Library of Congress.

2011 Portland musician Esperanza Spalding becomes the first jazz musician to win the "Best New Artist" category at the Grammy Awards.

2013 More than 68,000 fans at a Seattle Seahawks football game set a Guinness World Record for loudest crowd noise, at an ear-splitting 137.6 decibels!

2020 Marilyn Strickland is elected to the U.S. House of Representatives, becoming the first African American to represent Washington in Congress. She is also one of the first three Korean American women in the House of Representatives.

Dozens of lighthouses stand tall along the shore and on islands and sea rocks. One of the most famous is the TILLAMOOK ROCK LIGHTHOUSE, nicknamed "Terrible Tilly" because of the rough seas surrounding it.

CRUISE SHIPS sail up and down the coast, carrying tourists who explore the region's glaciers and fjords while spotting whales and other ocean creatures.

Giant KELP FORESTS grow beneath the waves. Reaching lengths of up to 200 feet, the kelp provides a habitat for sea otters and other ocean animals.

The Pacific Coast

The Pacific Northwest just wouldn't be the same without the Pacific! The world's largest ocean meets the land in a rugged coastline that stretches for more than a thousand miles from California up to Alaska. The coast is marked by fjords and bays and, in many places, mountains go nearly up to the water's edge. There are also countless islands, ranging in size from giant Vancouver to small, uninhabited rocks.

The American merchant Captain Robert Gray explored the mouth of the COLUMBIA RIVER in 1792 and named the river after his ship, the *Columbia Rediviva*.

More than a dozen different species of WHALES, DOLPHINS, and PORPOISES are regularly seen in the waters off the PNW coast.

The 4-mile-long ASTORIA-MEGLER BRIDGE spans the mouth of the Columbia River in an area once called the "graveyard of the Pacific" because of how many ships had been wrecked there. A little south along the coast you'll find the wrecked remains of the *Peter Iredale*, a ship that ran aground in 1906.

In winter, crested PUFFINS fly over the ocean, looking for food. Their bright orange-red bills and tufts of yellow feathers make them easy to spot!

Canada has more coastline than any other country. While most of its waters are too cold for surfing, brave souls in the coastal town of TOFINO don wetsuits to tackle the waves!

In Astoria, Oregon, the 125-foot ASTORIA COLUMN stands watch on the coast. Climb the 164 steps to the top to get great views out to sea, or stay on the ground to admire the artworks telling the history of the area.

You usually associate sand dunes with deserts, but the massive OREGON DUNES provided the inspiration for author Frank Herbert's famous *Dune* series, set on the desert planet of Arrakis.

When WILLIAM CLARK first sighted the Pacific on November 7, 1805 he wrote in his journal "Ocian in view! O! The joy."

Spectacular Sports

If you love the outdoors, then the PNW is the place for you. But it's more than just a wilderness—there are all kinds of sporting events and team sports to enjoy!

How many PROFESSIONAL SPORTS TEAMS in the PNW can you name? The last page of this book has a list of some of them.

At the 1968 Olympics, Portland native Dick Fosbury stunned the world when he went over the high jump bar headfirst and backward! No one had ever jumped like this before, but Fosbury won gold and all modern high jumpers now use the "FOSBURY FLOP."

Vancouver hosted the WINTER OLYMPICS in 2010, and Canadian athletes set a record by winning 14 gold medals. Both the men's and women's Canadian ice hockey teams took gold!

Although the SEATTLE MARINERS set a record in 2001 by winning 116 games, they remain the only current MLB team never to have made an appearance in the World Series. Better luck next season!

Canada has TWO OFFICIAL SPORTS: lacrosse in the summer and ice hockey in the winter.

Each year the CASCADIA CUP is awarded to the best men's professional soccer team in the PNW. The Portland Timbers, Seattle Sounders, and Vancouver Whitecaps fight it out to see who ends up with the trophy.

In the Oregon town of Hood River, WINDSURFERS make use of the perfect conditions on the Columbia River. It's such a great site that people call it the "windsurfing capital of the world!"

Have you ever played PICKLEBALL? This fun backyard sport uses paddles, a whiffle ball, and a badminton net. It was invented in Washington and is now the state's official sport.

Every Sunday night in Portland, daredevils climb onto tiny children's bikes and zoom down a steep hill at high speed. The course starts at the city zoo, so this wild ride is called "ZOOBOMBING!"

The extremely dedicated fans of the Portland Trail Blazers NBA team are said to suffer from "BLAZERMANIA." From 1977 through 1995, they set a record of 814 consecutive sold-out home games!

In the 1960s, Oregon track coach Bill Bowerman helped popularize JOGGING as a hobby. He was obsessed with trying to create the perfect running shoe and ruined his wife's waffle iron trying to make a new kind of sole.

You've heard of medieval knights JOUSTING on horseback, but in Seattle, riders do it on specially modified tall bikes!

Ellensburg, Washington, is where you'll find one of the world's rarest GEMSTONES: the Ellensburg blue agate. These beautiful blue stones were prized by the Kittitas Indigenous people, and only chiefs were allowed to wear them.

The plateau includes about 500 miles of the COLUMBIA RIVER, which cuts deep gorges into the rock, as well as smaller rivers that feed into it, such as the Snake and the Yakima.

Visit GINKGO PETRIFIED FOREST STATE PARK in Washington to see over 50 different species of trees that have been turned to stone, including ginkgo (of course), walnut, maple, redwood, and Douglas fir.

Rich volcanic soils make the plateau a FARMING POWERHOUSE. Wheat is the main crop, but farmers also grow potatoes, onions, and even watermelons. The region also produces huge quantities of apples—in fact, Washington produces more than 60 percent of the country's apples.

The Columbia Plateau

Let's travel east from the coast until we reach the Columbia Plateau. People think of the PNW as being cool, wet, and mountainous, but the plateau is proof that there's more to it than that! This huge area of high, dry, and relatively flat land takes up most of eastern Washington and stretches into Oregon and Idaho. It's a rural region with many small towns but few large cities, and it's become an important agricultural center where lots of crops are grown.

The plateau formed millions of years ago from huge amounts of VOLCANIC LAVA. The plateau is so big (about the size of Colorado) and its rocks are so thick that it contains more rock than some of the world's largest mountain ranges!

Many farmers on the plateau owe their success to the GRAND COULEE DAM, which was built on the Columbia River in 1941. It supplies water for growing crops, as well as generating hydroelectric power for homes and businesses.

"CHANNELED SCABLANDS" might sound like something you'd find on your knee after falling off your bike, but in fact this is a special type of landscape found in the Columbia Plateau. The scablands formed when floodwaters eroded the rock, leaving deep channels and holes.

You'll see plenty of WIND TURBINES as you travel through the plateau. The region gets a lot of wind, and it produces 83 percent of all the wind power in Washington, Oregon, and Idaho.

The Columbia Plateau is nestled between the ROCKY MOUNTAINS to the east and the CASCADE RANGE to the west.

The plateau is the ancestral home to many INDIGENOUS PEOPLES, including the Nimiipuu (Nez Perce) peoples and the Yakama peoples, who have lived as environmental stewards of the region for thousands of years. Many of the place names in the region come from their languages.

The dry grasslands of the plateau provide the PERFECT HABITAT for small mammals such as jackrabbits and the Washington ground squirrel, as well as ground-nesting birds such as grouse.

Trees & Flowers

The people of the PNW are proud of their trees—
so proud, in fact, that they put a Douglas fir right in
the middle of their flag! Trees are a big part of the
region's identity, and Washington and Oregon alone
have 16 national forests between them. But it's not
just about towering trees: a huge range of flowers,
vegetables, and other plants also grow here.

One of the most common
wildflowers in the PNW is
the CAMASSIA (also called
the quamash). They send up
spikes covered in star-shaped
bluish-purple flowers.

Coast Salish Indigenous
peoples used the
bark of the PACIFIC
DOGWOOD to treat
infections and the
wood to make tools.
They know the tree
as "kwi'txulhp."

Many of the trees found in the PNW
are real whoppers: the DOUGLAS FIR
and the SITKA SPRUCE can grow to
more than 300 feet. But it's the COAST
REDWOOD that takes the prize as the
tallest. Hyperion, a redwood growing
in northern California, stands at a
staggering 380 feet, making it the
world's tallest living tree!

Trees are so popular in Oregon that even
the state fossil is a tree! METASEQUOIA
grew throughout the region during
the late Cretaceous period, when
Tyrannosaurus rex ruled the land.

The pink blooms of the
COAST RHODODENDRON are
Washington's state flower.

Washington is famous for its APPLES, and
the state's vast orchards grow dozens
of different varieties—from the familiar
Red Delicious and Granny Smith to
more unusual breeds such as Ambrosia,
Rosalynn, and Crimson Delight.

Oregon may be known for wine, but you can't make wine from the OREGON GRAPE. That's because it's not really a grape at all! This shrub produces tart blue berries that some people make into jam, and its yellow blooms are Oregon's state flower.

The temperate rain forests of the PNW are the perfect habitat for plants such as the WESTERN SWORD FERN. The little leaflets on its long fronds look like tiny green daggers!

The Haida people use the wood of the WESTERN RED CEDAR to make totem poles, but only after performing a ceremony of gratitude to the tree.

Washington's state vegetable, the delicious WALLA WALLA SWEET ONION, only grows in the Walla Walla valley. Farmers carefully bred this onion over many years to end up with a vegetable that's big, round, and sweet. Even better, they won't make you cry when you cut them!

Idaho's state flower is the SYRINGA, also known as "Lewis's mock-orange" after the explorer Meriwether Lewis. This shrub's fragrant white flowers smell of orange blossom—with a hint of pineapple!

All hail the humble POTATO! This crop grows well in the climate of the PNW, and it's the state vegetable of both Idaho and Oregon.

The clue is in the name—the temperate rain forest gets up to 167 inches of RAINFALL every year. Compare that to Los Angeles, which gets only 14 inches per year!

The mighty ROOSEVELT ELK is named for President Theodore Roosevelt, to honor his efforts to preserve the animal's native habitat. As they graze on the forest floor, the elk clear space for new plants to grow.

PREDATORS such as lynx, mountain lions, bobcats, and bears prowl through the forest as they hunt for food.

A temperate rain forest STAYS COOL even in the summer, rarely reaching temperatures over 80°F.

Looking very much like an overripe banana, the brightly colored BANANA SLUG oozes along the forest floor. The biggest ones can grow to 10 inches long!

A fallen tree trunk called a NURSE LOG can have mosses, fungi, and young trees growing on it, as well as insects and other small animals living inside it.

Over the decades, huge areas of rainforest have been lost to LOGGING, but many of the remaining forests are protected.

Did you know that some squirrels can fly? Well, they can glide. At night, NORTHERN FLYING SQUIRRELS zoom from tree to tree, stretching out their four limbs to use special flaps of skin as wings.

The FOREST FLOOR is covered in a thick layer of dead and decaying leaves, tree trunks, and animal remains. They provide nutrients that help plants grow.

Most of the trees in the temperate rain forest are CONIFERS, which means they produce cones. Species include the Douglas fir, Sitka spruce, coast redwood, and western red cedar. Some of these trees can live for many hundreds of years.

Amphibians such as NEWTS AND SALAMANDERS scurry along the forest floor.

Cool Rain Forests

When you hear the words "rain forest," you probably think of somewhere hot and steamy like the Amazon, with parrots swooping from tree to tree. But the PNW is home to a rarer kind of habitat, where trees and heavy rain combine with cooler temperatures to create a "temperate rain forest." Stretching along the Pacific coast, all the way from Alaska to northern California, the PNW's temperate rain forest is the largest in the world. It's home to a huge range of plants and animals.

Below the soil, a huge UNDERGROUND NETWORK of fungi connects the roots of different trees and lets them pass on nutrients.

Museums & Attractions

There's plenty to do in the Pacific Northwest! With everything from nail-biting theme park rides to quirky museums and historic sites, you'll never be bored in this fascinating region.

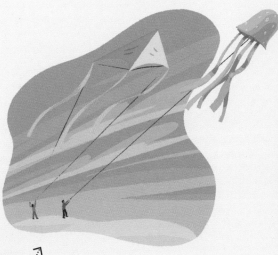

Go to Oregon's Evergreen Aviation & Space Museum to see the Spruce Goose, the largest FLYING BOAT ever built. It's made almost entirely of wood—though despite the name it's mainly birch, not spruce!

Rides at northern Idaho's Silverwood Theme Park include a LOG FLUME that is the real deal! The attraction is based on the actual log flumes that once carried trees from the PNW's forests to sawmills and lumber yards.

When a gold rush hit British Columbia in the 1860s, the town of Barkerville sprang up almost overnight. Now you can see what life in a GOLD RUSH TOWN was like by touring its historic buildings—more than 125 of them in total. You can also learn to pan for gold, and maybe strike it rich!

The Pacific coast's reputation for being windy makes it the perfect location for the WORLD KITE MUSEUM. Every August the museum runs an International Kite Festival, when the skies are filled with colorful kites from around the world.

Put on your hard hat and hop on board a mine train to travel through underground tunnels at the BRITANNIA MINE MUSEUM. In the 1930s, this massive mine produced nearly one-fifth of the world's copper.

Did you know that Canada has a castle? CRAIGHDARROCH CASTLE was built in the 1880s by a rich Scottish coal baron as a way to show off his enormous wealth.

Take a selfie with the world's largest rubber chicken at the RUBBER CHICKEN MUSEUM in Seattle. Why have so many comedians used these bizarre toys as props? You'll have to visit to find out!

At the SEATTLE PINBALL MUSEUM, you don't just admire the vintage pinball machines—you can play on them as much as you like. Now that's a real hands-on exhibit!

If you love creepy-crawlies then the BREMERTON BUG & REPTILE MUSEUM is the place for you! Explore a giant ant farm and get up close and personal with snakes, lizards, and insects.

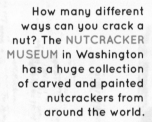

How many different ways can you crack a nut? The NUTCRACKER MUSEUM in Washington has a huge collection of carved and painted nutcrackers from around the world.

The humble hammer gets star treatment at the HAMMER MUSEUM in Haines, Alaska, where more than 2,000 examples are on show. The biggest is 20 feet high!

At the Spark Museum, you can stand your hair on end with static electricity. The bravest visitors enter the "Cage of Doom" to be STRUCK BY LIGHTNING from the "Mega Zapper." Truly shocking!

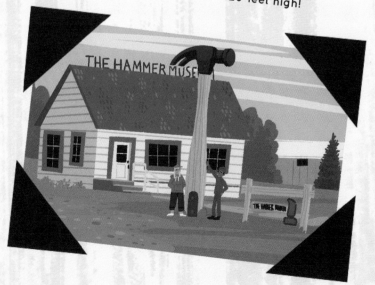

Vancouver is nicknamed "HOLLYWOOD NORTH" because so many films and television shows are filmed here. It's not unusual to spot filming taking place as you walk around!

Do you have a good head for heights? Try the CAPILANO SUSPENSION BRIDGE, a narrow pedestrian bridge suspended high above Capilano Canyon in the north of the city. Just don't look down!

The city of Vancouver sits on a PENINSULA, surrounded on three sides by the waters of the Strait of Georgia. Across the strait lies an island the size of Maryland, also called Vancouver.

Fleets of FERRIES AND WATER TAXIS carry cars and passengers between the mainland and the nearby islands.

GRANVILLE IS

Vancouver has WELCOMED IMMIGRANTS from around the world, including many from Asia. About half of the city's population have a first language other than English.

Winters in Vancouver can be very rainy, but when it rains in the city, it snows in the mountains. That makes it the perfect base for SKIING, SNOWBOARDING, and SNOWSHOEING, a kind of hiking in the snow.

NET

Once voted the best park in the world, STANLEY PARK is home to half a million trees, as well as an aquarium, an outdoor theater, and a miniature railroad. You can also see a collection of totem poles carved by the region's Indigenous peoples, including the Kwakwaka'wakw and the Haida.

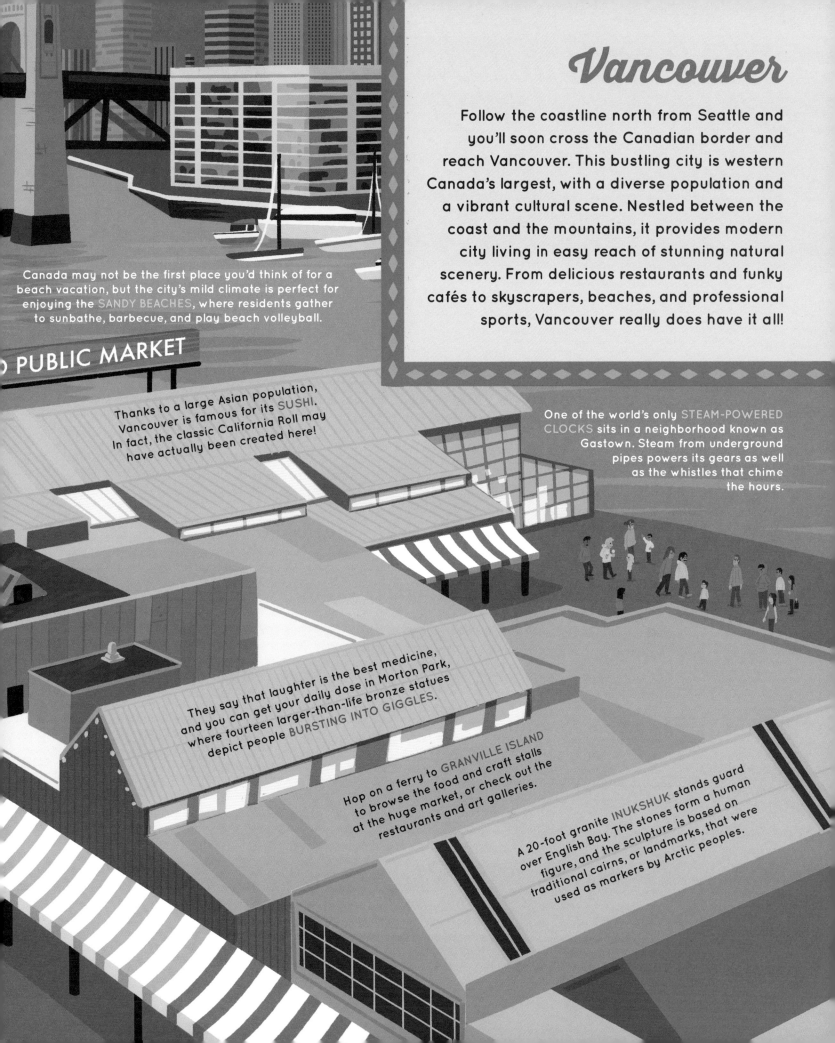

Vancouver

Follow the coastline north from Seattle and you'll soon cross the Canadian border and reach Vancouver. This bustling city is western Canada's largest, with a diverse population and a vibrant cultural scene. Nestled between the coast and the mountains, it provides modern city living in easy reach of stunning natural scenery. From delicious restaurants and funky cafés to skyscrapers, beaches, and professional sports, Vancouver really does have it all!

Canada may not be the first place you'd think of for a beach vacation, but the city's mild climate is perfect for enjoying the SANDY BEACHES, where residents gather to sunbathe, barbecue, and play beach volleyball.

PUBLIC MARKET

Thanks to a large Asian population, Vancouver is famous for its SUSHI. In fact, the classic California Roll may have actually been created here!

One of the world's only STEAM-POWERED CLOCKS sits in a neighborhood known as Gastown. Steam from underground pipes powers its gears as well as the whistles that chime the hours.

They say that laughter is the best medicine, and you can get your daily dose in Morton Park, where fourteen larger-than-life bronze statues depict people BURSTING INTO GIGGLES.

Hop on a ferry to GRANVILLE ISLAND to browse the food and craft stalls at the huge market, or check out the restaurants and art galleries.

A 20-foot granite INUKSHUK stands guard over English Bay. The stones form a human figure, and the sculpture is based on traditional cairns, or landmarks, that were used as markers by Arctic peoples.

Food, Glorious Food

Food in the Pacific Northwest is often based on fresh local ingredients and many dishes represent a fusion of different traditions, including Asian and Indigenous American. The quirky range means that everyone can find something delicious!

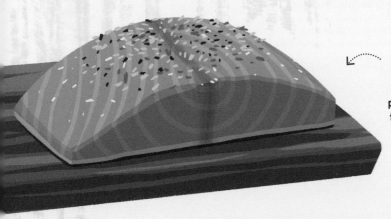

The PNW is famous for SALMON, and you'll find it on menus everywhere. It's often cooked on a soaked plank of cedar wood on the grill. This technique originated with the area's Indigenous peoples and gives the salmon a smoky flavor.

The humble TATER TOT was invented by the Oregon company Ore-Ida in the 1950s. Many PNW bars and restaurants now offer "loaded" tots. These include "totchos," a version of nachos using tater tots in place of tortilla chips.

Go to a sports stadium in Seattle and you'll find fans munching on SEATTLE DOGS. These hot dogs are slathered in cream cheese and topped with grilled onions.

The Canadian city of Nanaimo gives its name to a creamy, chocolatey treat. Made with wafer, nuts, coconut, custard, and chocolate, no one quite knows who first invented the NANAIMO BAR, but it's so popular that it was featured on a postage stamp!

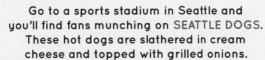

Nearly all of the HAZELNUTS grown in the United States come from Oregon. People snack on plain hazelnuts, crush them to make a coating for fish, toss them in salads, and of course cover them in delicious chocolate.

If you can't decide between steak and fries, why not try a dish that gives you the best of both? FINGER STEAKS are an Idaho specialty: strips of steak that have been breaded and deep-fried.

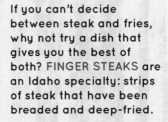

People along the Pacific coast have eaten BERRIES for thousands of years. The huckleberry is Idaho's state fruit, and people throughout the PNW use them to make jam, honey, syrup, and even taffy!

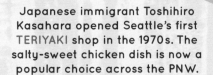

Japanese immigrant Toshihiro Kasahara opened Seattle's first TERIYAKI shop in the 1970s. The salty-sweet chicken dish is now a popular choice across the PNW.

Vancouver's many sushi restaurants are the best place to find a B.C. ROLL, which contains barbecued salmon and cucumber wrapped in seaweed and rice. It was invented in 1974 by sushi chef Hidekazu Tojo.

Coffee plants don't grow in the PNW, but ever since the first STARBUCKS opened in Seattle in the 1960s, coffee—and coffee shops—have become a staple of the entire region.

Feeling a bit more adventurous than chocolate or vanilla? AKUTAQ, also known as Alaskan ice cream, is a traditional dish of the region's Indigenous peoples. It's made from animal fat, fish, and fresh berries, all whipped together to make a foamy treat. Or you could try SXUSEM, an Indigenous treat from British Columbia made from soapberries whipped with water and sugar.

The Pacific coast is known for its seafood, including DUNGENESS CRAB. Its meat is sweeter than lobster, and people love to mix it with mayonnaise, celery, and green onions, then serve in a brioche roll.

The deep COLUMBIA RIVER GORGE splits the Cascades in two and forms part of the border between Washington and Oregon.

We know many of the mountains by the names that British and American explorers gave them, but they have older INDIGENOUS NAMES, such as "Tahoma" or "Tacoma" for Mount Rainier and "Pahto" for Mount Adams. The original Klickitat name for Mount St. Helens, "Louwala-Clough," means "smoking mountain."

The mountains take their name from a stretch of WHITEWATER RAPIDS known as the "Cascades of the Columbia," which were a dangerous obstacle to early river travelers.

Settlers following the Oregon Trail found the Cascades blocking their way. Some loaded their belongings onto rafts and braved the rapids of the Columbia River, while others drove their cattle over the mountains via the LOLO PASS, an old Indigenous trading route.

Climb a peak in the Cascades and you'll start in a forest, but as you get higher you'll see only moss and lichen—and on the highest peaks there are NO PLANTS AT ALL!

The Cascades are the ancestral home of many different Indigenous groups, such as the CHELAN PEOPLE, who left pictographs (rock paintings) on the region's cliffs.

At 14,410 feet, MOUNT RAINIER holds the record as the highest peak in the Cascades. It was once even taller, before an eruption more than 5,000 years ago made its top collapse!

The Cascades

The towering Cascade Range forms the backbone of the Pacific Northwest, stretching from the southern part of British Columbia all the way down to northern California. But don't let the scenic beauty of the Cascades fool you! They've been the site of violent volcanic eruptions, and there could be more in the future. These snow-capped mountains are part of the Ring of Fire—a belt of volcanoes and earthquake zones that form a ring around the Pacific Ocean.

When mountaintop snow melts, it feeds fast-flowing streams and rivers that are an important source of HYDROELECTRIC POWER in the region.

The southern end of the range is marked by LASSEN PEAK in northern California—a massive lava dome volcano that produced a series of eruptions from 1914-1921.

VOLCANIC SOIL is great for growing plants, so the land near the Cascades is often used for farming.

MOUNTAIN GOATS live on the steep slopes of the Cascades, using their cloven hooves to grip the rock as they jump from crag to crag.

PACKS OF WOLVES once roamed the Cascades, until human activity nearly drove them to extinction in the 1930s. Now, as an endangered species, they are protected and are beginning to reclaim some of their hunting grounds in Washington.

Are you brave enough to SKI ON AN ACTIVE VOLCANO? Oregon's Mount Hood is the site of a popular ski resort, but luckily this volcano hasn't erupted for more than 200 years.

Amazing Animals

With a range of habitats, from coastal waters to mountains and rain forests, it's no wonder that the Pacific Northwest also has a huge range of animal species. Some of them are found nowhere else on Earth! Meet a few of our favorite feathered, furry, fishy, and creepy-crawly friends.

The OLYMPIC MARMOT is Washington's state endemic mammal, meaning that it is only found there, and nowhere else! The marmots live in family groups, greeting each other by touching noses.

Oregon's nickname is "The Beaver State," because huge numbers of BEAVERS once lived along the state's many streams. They were nearly hunted to extinction for their fur, but are now recovering. Beavers are Canada's national animal and appear on the Canadian nickel.

Explore Idaho's damp evergreen forests and you might spot the official state amphibian—the IDAHO GIANT SALAMANDER. Sometimes growing to over a foot long, they come out at night when it is rainy and warm.

American symbols don't come any more iconic than the BALD EAGLE, and these majestic birds are a common sight in the PNW, where they nest in large trees.

People in the PNW have been catching SALMON for thousands of years. Every year salmon return from the ocean to the freshwater rivers and streams where they hatched, to breed.

ORCAS, also known as killer whales, are the superstars of the PNW. People come from all over to see them, and they're an important symbol in Indigenous cultures.

Blue animals are fairly rare, but the MOUNTAIN BLUEBIRD isn't afraid to show its colors! Females are grayish-brown with a few blue highlights while males are blue all over. They're often spotted in grasslands in Idaho, where they are the official state bird.

Both brown and black bears live in the PNW, but British Columbia's official mammal is the SPIRIT BEAR. These white bears might be easily mistaken for polar bears, but they're actually a subspecies of black bear with a genetic quirk that can make their fur white. Their rarity and beauty has made them an important part of First Nations mythology.

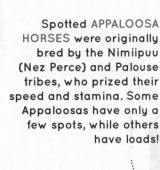

Spotted APPALOOSA HORSES were originally bred by the Nimiipuu (Nez Perce) and Palouse tribes, who prized their speed and stamina. Some Appaloosas have only a few spots, while others have loads!

SEA OTTERS live in the kelp forests off the Pacific coast. They sleep while floating on their backs, holding hands with other otters to form groups called "rafts." This helps them stay warm and stops them from drifting away. Cute!

The ancient forests of the PNW were once home to large numbers of the NORTHERN SPOTTED OWL, but logging has pushed these nocturnal predators to the brink of extinction.

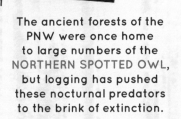

The official state amphibian of Washington, the PACIFIC CHORUS FROG, also known as the Pacific tree frog, can change color to blend in with its surroundings as the seasons change.

The lake holds nearly 5 TRILLION GALLONS of water—that's enough to fill 7.4 million Olympic-sized swimming pools!

The lake's beautiful CLEAR BLUE WATERS all come from rainfall and snowfall. There are no rivers to bring water to the lake or carry it away.

The cone-shaped island in the middle of the lake is called WIZARD ISLAND. After the eruption that created the crater, this island formed from new eruptions of lava. It's like a mini-volcano, and it last erupted 4,800 years ago.

The lake is home to a population of MAZAMA NEWTS, a species of semi-aquatic salamander. They live mainly on land but return to the water to breed.

See if you can spot the OLD MAN OF THE LAKE, a 30-foot log of mountain hemlock that floats upright in the lake. Only the top three feet are exposed above the surface. The log is at least 450 years old and moves slowly through the lake's waters, covering about a mile per day.

The park is centered around MOUNT MAZAMA, a volcano that once stood about 12,000 feet high. Its name in the language of the local Klamath people is "Tum-sum-ne."

The HUGE CRATER is about 6 miles wide and 0.7 miles deep. The lake that fills it has an average depth of 1,943 feet, making it the deepest lake in the United States.

Fields of UNDERWATER MOSS form a ring around the lake's rim. Moss needs sunlight to make food, and it's only the exceptional clarity of the water that allows it to survive here at depths of more than 400 feet.

The crater formed after an ENORMOUS VOLCANIC ERUPTION about 7,700 years ago, which made the top of Mount Mazama collapse in on itself. The mountain's highest point is now just 8,151 feet.

Indigenous people were using Mount Mazama as a temporary camping site at the time of the eruption, and their legends tell of the event. Archaeologists have found INDIGENOUS ARTIFACTS buried under layers of ash.

Crater Lake is located in KLAMATH COUNTY, which takes its name from the Klamath (also spelled Clamitte) people who have lived in the region for thousands of years. Their name for the lake is "Giiwas."

Crater Lake National Park

The Pacific Northwest has no shortage of national and state parks, all offering a chance to get up close and personal with the region's stunning scenery. Each park is unique in its own way, but Crater Lake is really something special. Oregon's only national park, this special spot is the site of one of the world's deepest—and most beautiful—lakes. Its location in the crater of an extinct volcano gives it extra wow factor!

Cool Inventions

There have always been people who aren't afraid to dream big. Their creative ideas have led to incredible and never-been-seen-before products and techniques. Here are just a few of the many inventions from the innovative Pacific Northwest.

Washington native Floyd Paxton invented the BREAD BAG CLIP on an airplane when he wanted to close a bag of peanuts. He whittled one from an old credit card, then started a company that still produces them by the millions!

One of the first INKJET PRINTERS was developed in the PNW, by Hewlett-Packard. These printers use heat to shoot ink through a tiny nozzle—like a much, much smaller version of the volcanoes that dominate the area!

Cultures all around the world play games where people use their feet to keep a small object from hitting the ground. One of the most popular of these objects, the HACKY SACK, was invented by two friends in Oregon in 1972.

After PNW sportsman Eddie Bauer was nearly killed by a case of hypothermia in 1935, he invented the first DOWN-FILLED PARKA. He went on to design versions for mountaineers and Second World War pilots.

Wanting to find a way for friends who lived without electricity to be able to read and study in the evening, 15-year-old Ann Makosinski from British Columbia invented a BATTERY-FREE FLASHLIGHT. It uses heat from the palm of the user's hand to generate power.

Back in the day, you had one faucet for hot water and another for cold. After burning his hand on a hot faucet, Seattle local Alfred Moen invented one with only one handle. This MIXING FAUCET made it easier to get the temperature just right.

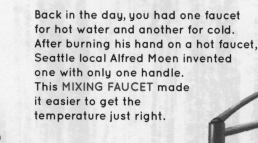

Washington is the home of MICROSOFT, so anyone who has ever booted up a Windows-based computer has been using an invention from the Pacific Northwest!

Before Dr E. Donnall Thomas and his team at the Seattle Public Health Hospital developed BONE MARROW TRANSPLANTATION, there were few effective ways to treat leukemia and other blood cancers. Their amazing work has saved many thousands of lives.

Many of the world's electric guitar legends make use of another home-grown PNW invention: the WHAMMY BAR. This ingenious little add-on lets guitarists change the pitch to create cool-sounding vibrating effects.

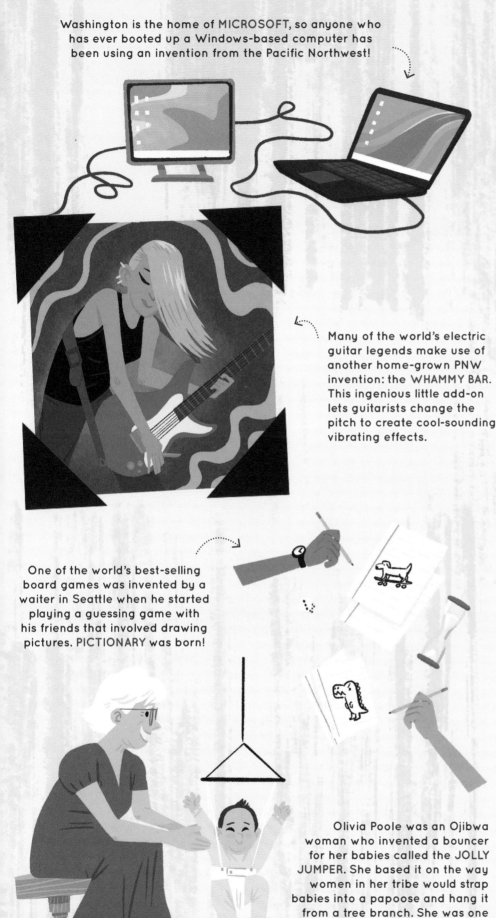

So simple, but so essential, the EGG CARTON was invented by Joseph Coyle in British Columbia in 1911. He overheard someone complaining about a delivery of broken eggs, then invented a carton with individual pockets. Problem solved!

One of the world's best-selling board games was invented by a waiter in Seattle when he started playing a guessing game with his friends that involved drawing pictures. PICTIONARY was born!

Olivia Poole was an Ojibwa woman who invented a bouncer for her babies called the JOLLY JUMPER. She based it on the way women in her tribe would strap babies into a papoose and hang it from a tree branch. She was one of the first Indigenous women in Canada to patent an invention.

Spokane

If you hop in a car and drive due east from Seattle, after a couple hundred miles you'll reach Spokane. It may be only a fraction of the size of Seattle, Vancouver, or Portland, but Spokane is the unofficial capital of the Inland Northwest—a large region centered around eastern Washington. For the people who call this sparsely populated rural area home, Spokane is the nearest big city. Its stunning riverfront, charming historic buildings, and beautiful parks make it well worth a visit.

Make the most of the Spokane River with a visit to RIVERFRONT PARK, where you can play in a fountain, catch an open-air concert, ride an antique carousel, or even climb into a cable car for a jaw-dropping trip over the falls!

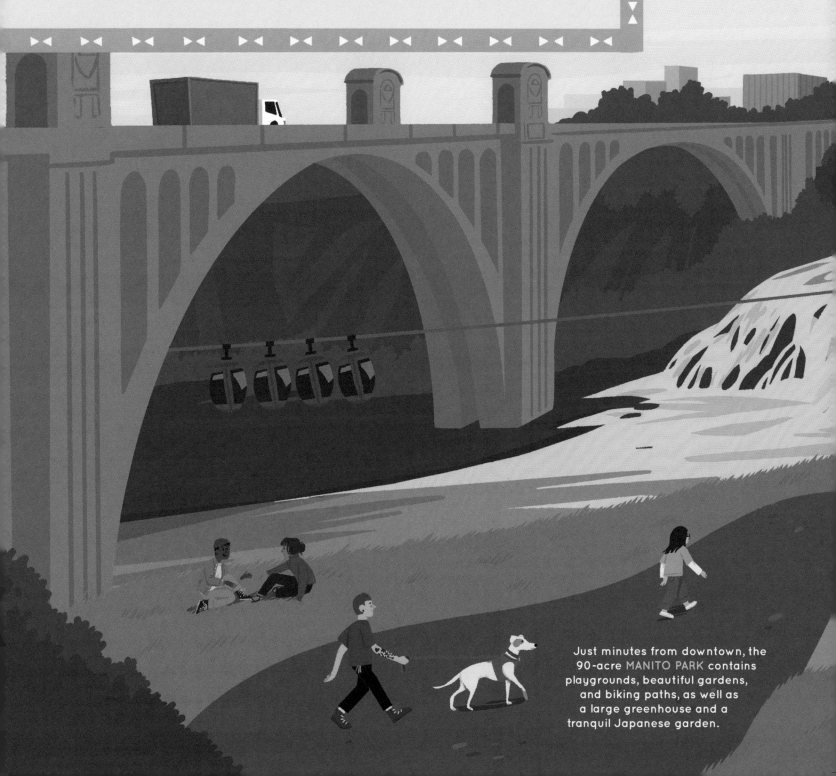

Just minutes from downtown, the 90-acre MANITO PARK contains playgrounds, beautiful gardens, and biking paths, as well as a large greenhouse and a tranquil Japanese garden.

Calling all dads! Did you know that FATHER'S DAY got its start in Spokane? In 1910, a local resident suggested that dads were just as deserving of a special day as mothers were . . . and the rest is history!

The CATHEDRAL OF ST. JOHN THE EVANGELIST looks like something you'd see in a quaint English town. This ancient-looking stone cathedral was actually built between 1925 and 1961.

Spokane takes its name from the SPOKANE TRIBE who lived along the banks of what we now call the Spokane River. They fished for salmon and other fish, and hunted and gathered in the surrounding area.

Not many cities can claim to have a waterfall thundering right through the downtown area! Divided into upper and lower sections, the SPOKANE FALLS are especially impressive in May, when melting snow makes the river even more powerful.

Spokane was a thriving young city on the rise when the GREAT FIRE OF 1889 destroyed the downtown area. But the residents built it back bigger, better, and safer.

Spokane may be a long way from the Pacific coast, but you can still get up close and personal with sea life at the BLUE ZOO AQUARIUM. Are you brave enough to pat a stingray?

The SALMON CHIEF STATUE stands along the river near the historic Monroe Street Bridge. The figure on horseback holds up a salmon to bless it, reminding us that the area was once an important fishing ground.

Marmots are large rodents that usually live in the wilderness, but a population of YELLOW-BELLIED MARMOTS call Spokane home. They're often seen on rocky riverbanks in the downtown area.

Fun Festivals

The Pacific Northwest is overflowing with festivals that celebrate the region's people, history, and produce, as well as some that are just a little bit wacky. From flowers and hot chocolate to motorized bathtubs and garlic ice cream, there's definitely something for everyone.

If FLOWERS are your thing, make sure to hit the Skagit Valley Tulip Festival near Seattle in April, then move on to the Portland Rose Festival in late May and the Willamette Valley Lavender Festival in July. They all sound blooming amazing!

Every October, seafood lovers descend on the town of Shelton, Washington for its annual OYSTERFEST, which features the West Coast Oyster Shucking Championships! People compete to see how fast they can remove the tasty oysters from their shells.

Celebrate Indigenous culture at the GATHERING AT THE FALLS POWWOW in Spokane. This festival features traditional dance, drumming, and music, and continues a tradition that goes back many generations.

At the ELEPHANT GARLIC FESTIVAL in North Plains, Oregon, you can watch parades, live music, and the annual crowning of the Garlic Queen and Garlic King. You can even try garlic ice cream if you're brave enough!

A famous 1950 UFO sighting in McMinnville, Oregon, led to the founding of the MCMENAMINS UFO FESTIVAL. Ufologists—that's people who study UFOs—come from far and wide to swap theories and evidence.

Portland's annual PEDALPALOOZA festival is a celebration of cycling. There are dozens of different themed bike rides to choose from—some include bells or other noisemakers, and others involve costumes or even no clothes at all!

There's nothing like a cup of hot chocolate on a cold winter's day! During Vancouver's annual HOT CHOCOLATE FESTIVAL you can try a huge range of different flavors from cafés throughout the city.

In Nanaimo, BC, brave sailors strap motors to bathtubs and set off on a long and grueling course through the waters around the city. It's all part of the annual NANAIMO MARINE FESTIVAL.

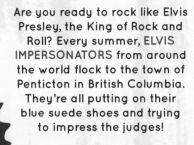

Are you ready to rock like Elvis Presley, the King of Rock and Roll? Every summer, ELVIS IMPERSONATORS from around the world flock to the town of Penticton in British Columbia. They're all putting on their blue suede shoes and trying to impress the judges!

All hail the humble lentil! These legume superfoods have been grown in eastern Washington for many years, and the town of Pullman hosts the NATIONAL LENTIL FESTIVAL. The highlight is the lentil chili cook-off—with a free bowl for every spectator, of course!

How much strawberry shortcake could you eat? Washington's BELLEVUE STRAWBERRY FESTIVAL honors an important local crop. There are contests, pony rides, craft stalls, classic cars . . . and of course, the chance to stuff your face with delicious strawberries!

Real Vikings never made it as far as Washington, but the people of Poulsbo hold a VIKING FEST every May to celebrate the Scandinavian heritage of some of its early settlers. There's music, dancing, battle demonstrations, and even a contest to see who is the strongest!

Islands

It's no surprise that a largely coastal region like the Pacific Northwest is home to many islands. They run all along the Pacific coast and range in size from Vancouver Island—about the size of Maryland—to numerous tiny uninhabited rocks. Although a few of the islands have large populations, most of the others are known for their pristine natural beauty. It would take a lifetime to visit them all!

The islands of Alaska's Alexander Archipelago are actually the tops of a submerged mountain range! The islands are covered in thick evergreen forests and temperate rain forest and make up part of the enormous TONGASS NATIONAL FOREST.

PRINCE OF WALES ISLAND in Alaska sits in fourth place on the list of largest islands in the U.S. Slightly larger than Delaware, it has a long, rugged coastline marked by bays, coves, and steep-sided fjords.

Conditions in the Pacific Ocean can be rough, so many ships follow the INSIDE PASSAGE instead. Offering calmer waters, this route weaves through the islands that hug the coast from Olympia, Washington to southern Alaska.

The HAIDA GWAII archipelago was once known as the Queen Charlotte Islands but reclaimed its Indigenous name in 2010. Its huge range of wildlife—some of it unique to the region—has led to its nickname: "Canada's Galápagos."

ALASKA

BRITISH COLUMBIA

ALEXANDER ARCHIPELAGO

PRINCE OF WALES ISLAND

INSIDE PASSAGE

HAIDA GWAII ARCHIPELAGO

VANCOUVER ISLAND is both the largest and the most populated of the islands along the PNW's coast. Its largest cities are Victoria and Nanaimo—the city of Vancouver is actually on the mainland!

VANCOUVER

SAN JUAN ISLANDS

WHIDBEY ISLAND

PUGET SOUND

SEATTLE

PORTLAND

VANCOUVER ISLAND

OREGON COAST

Islands can be isolated places, but a network of FERRIES connects some of the larger islands to each other and to the mainland.

Nestled in Puget Sound, between the Washington coast and the southern end of Vancouver Island, you'll find the SAN JUAN ISLANDS. This archipelago is made up of more than 400 islands and rocks, though only about a dozen are inhabited.

Located about 30 miles north of Seattle, WHIDBEY ISLAND is Washington's largest. People arrive by ferry or drive over the bridge to enjoy the island's charming small towns and scenic beauty.

The Coast Salish people have used CANOES for thousands of years to travel along rivers and between the islands of the PNW. Carved from a single cedar log, these craft were tough and durable. They were used to ferry people and cargo between settlements, as well as for carrying raiding parties.

Oregon has no large islands, but a string of more than 5,000 small rocks, reefs, and islets runs along its coastline. They are protected as a NATURE RESERVE and serve as a nesting site for over a million seabirds, as well as a place for seals and sea lions to rest and breed.

Change Makers

Countless brave and creative people from the Pacific Northwest have left their mark on the world. We've chosen just a small handful from the huge number of inspirational people that have called this region home. They're thinkers, artists, activists, athletes, and leaders, and they've all done amazing things.

Winning the Nobel Prize is a huge achievement, and winning it twice is something that only five people have ever done. One of them was Oregon native LINUS PAULING. He won the chemistry prize in 1954, then won the Nobel Peace Prize in 1962 for his campaign to ban the testing of nuclear weapons.

Washington native BILL GATES has changed the world, not once but twice! First, he used his programming skills and business sense to launch Microsoft, which helped power the personal computing revolution in the 1980s and 90s. And now he's using the fortune he made to fund programs that focus on improving health and education around the globe.

In 1908, LOLA GREENE BALDWIN blazed a trail for women everywhere when she became one of the first female police officers in the U.S. Her job as a Superintendent involved turning young women in Portland away from a life of crime and promoting laws designed to improve women's safety.

RYAN REYNOLDS is one of Hollywood's biggest stars, appearing in superhero blockbusters and providing voices for animated films. He's also made a documentary series about buying a soccer team in Wales and won awards in his native Canada for his charity work.

The Simpsons is the longest-running animated series on U.S. television. It was the brainchild of Portland cartoonist MATT GROENING, who began his career drawing comic strips. After the success of *The Simpsons*, he went on to create another animated series called *Futurama*.

On any list of the best guitarists in rock history, you're sure to find JIMI HENDRIX. Born in Seattle, he used his guitar—strung upside-down to accommodate his left-handedness—in ways that no one had before. He mixed rock with blues, jazz, and soul to create truly original music.

Generations of American children grew up reading books by Oregon native BEVERLY CLEARY. Her characters, such as Ramona Quimby, were instantly relatable, and she tackled issues such as divorce, unemployment, and growing up with a huge dose of warmth, understanding, and charm

Most people knew CHIEF DAN GEORGE as an actor, but he was also a poet, a writer, and chief of the Tsleil-Waututh Nation. In 1970 he became the first Indigenous actor to be nominated for an Academy Award. Throughout his career he refused to play roles that showed Indigenous people in a negative way.

Oregon native STACY ALLISON began her mountain-climbing career in the Cascades. In 1988, she became the first American woman to reach the top of Mount Everest, where she posed with the pink plastic flamingo that was her team's mascot! She now works as a motivational speaker, encouraging others to follow their dreams.

Washington swimmer NATHAN ADRIAN won eight Olympic medals during his career—five of them gold. A specialist in the freestyle sprint and relay events, in 2019 he came back from treatment for testicular cancer to win two world championship gold medals.

JANET MCCLOUD was born on the Tulalip Reservation in Washington. In the 1960s and 70s she fought for the rights of Indigenous people to fish in their traditional waters by staging "fish-ins," where they defied game wardens to fish using traditional methods. For her efforts she was given the tribal name Yet-Si-Blue, meaning "the woman who talks."

The daughter of an enslaved woman, NETTIE CRAIG ASBERRY was a tireless fighter for equal rights, both for women and for the Black community. She was also an accomplished musician and music teacher. After moving to Tacoma in the 1890s, she set up the local chapter of the NAACP (National Association for the Advancement of Colored People) and fought against segregation.

WINONA LADUKE grew up in Ashland, Oregon, and studied economics at Harvard University. She became a tireless campaigner for the rights of Indigenous people to have control over their traditional homelands, so that they could protect their precious resources. She was the Green Party's candidate for vice president in 1996 and 2000.

You probably take your sense of smell for granted, but LINDA B. BUCK is one of the scientists who figured out how it actually works. Through years of research she discovered how smell affects memory and emotion, and in 2004, she won the Nobel Prize for her discoveries.

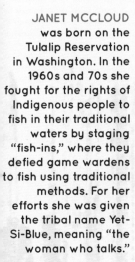

The Salish Sea

A vast inland sea forms the heart of the Pacific Northwest. Known as the Salish Sea, this body of water is a network of channels and waterways that separate islands and mainland. The best way to explore it is by boat, starting with the Strait of Juan de Fuca that leads into the sea from the Pacific Ocean. Then you can either head north into the Strait of Georgia, or south into Puget Sound. Whichever you choose, you'll see sparkling waters, beautiful beaches, rugged forested islands—and a few cities too.

For years, the names used for the different parts of the sea honored European explorers, colonizers, or rulers. In 2010 the entire sea was renamed in honor of the COAST SALISH PEOPLE who have lived along its shores for at least five thousand years.

The Salish Sea has a mix of SALTY OCEAN WATER AND FRESHWATER from various rivers, creating a unique habitat for marine animals and plants.

The Coast Salish are famous for their POTLATCHES. These ceremonies are marked by dancing, feasting, and gift-giving and are often held to celebrate marriages, births, or funerals.

Traditionally, the Coast Salish people spent the winters in permanent VILLAGES ALONG THE COAST, then moved around in the summer as they followed food sources, such as wild cherries and the bulbs of a plant called camas.

Seattle and Vancouver are the largest cities on the Salish Sea, but there are many others, including WASHINGTON'S CAPITAL CITY, Olympia.

There are HUNDREDS OF ISLANDS in the Salish Sea, including three main groups: the Discovery Islands, the Gulf Islands, and the San Juan Islands.

As well as beautiful kelp forests, you'll find EELGRASS growing in the shallow waters of the sea, providing a home for fish and crabs. An underwater microphone can pick up the bubbling sound that it makes as it releases life-giving oxygen into the water!

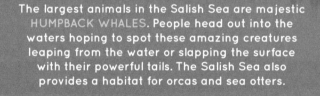

The largest animals in the Salish Sea are majestic HUMPBACK WHALES. People head out into the waters hoping to spot these amazing creatures leaping from the water or slapping the surface with their powerful tails. The Salish Sea also provides a habitat for orcas and sea otters.

Sea lions get their name because the males grow large, furry manes, and the STELLER SEA LIONS that live in the Salish Sea are the world's largest species.

Natural sponges are an ancient family of sea creatures. Scientists used to think that one species that formed HUGE UNDERWATER REEFS was long extinct, until some were discovered in the Salish Sea in 1987! The reefs grow in deep waters and can be the height of a six-story building.

The landscape of the Salish Sea was FORMED BY ICE SHEETS carving out deep channels in the land. When the ice finally retreated about 12,000 years ago, those channels filled with water to form the landscape that we see today.

The Awe of Mother Nature

Volcanoes, earthquakes, tornadoes, floods, fires, and heat waves: Mother Nature doesn't always give the Pacific Northwest an easy time. But no matter what nature brings, the locals know that the secret to staying safe is to always be prepared. They create plans with their families, gather supplies, pack emergency kits, and generally do everything they can to be ready for anything.

When the World Goes Boom

With a chain of volcanoes running through the PNW, it's no surprise that one of its biggest natural disasters in the area was an eruption. In March 1980, small earthquakes began to shake MOUNT ST. HELENS in Washington, followed by a series of small eruptions. Then, on May 18, the mountain exploded!

A powerful earthquake triggered a landslide that carried away the northern side of the mountain, while an eruption sent SUPER-HOT GAS AND ASH into the air and floods of mud and debris buried the surrounding area. Thousands of animals and 57 people lost their lives. Thankfully, none of the other volcanoes in the Cascades have erupted for over 100 years.

What's Shakin'?

Earthquakes are common in the PNW and they're usually fairly small, but a few big ones have really shaken things up! In 1700, an ENORMOUS EARTHQUAKE caused a tsunami that hit the coast of Japan, thousands of miles away. Ever since, the Coast Salish people have shared stories about an earthquake and a mighty flood that their ancestors survived.

Wild Winds

Many coastal regions get pounded by hurricanes, but the PNW is not one of them—the Pacific waters are just too cold for hurricanes to form. However, there have been several DESTRUCTIVE TORNADOES, including one that touched down near downtown Portland on April 5, 1972, before moving across the Columbia River to the neighboring city of Vancouver, Washington.

Too Hot to Handle

The PNW is known for its cool climate, but in 2021 a fierce HEAT WAVE hit the region. On June 29 the village of Lytton in British Columbia set the record for the highest ever temperature in Canada, at 121.3°F (49.6°C). The very next day the village was destroyed by a fire that swept through the area.

Water, Water Everywhere...

"Pineapple Express" might sound like a trendy juice bar, but it's the name given to a stream of warm, moist air that regularly flows from Hawaii to America's west coast. In 2021 it brought heavy rain to the PNW, causing FLOODS AND LANDSLIDES.

A Burning Question

The vast forests of the PNW are often destroyed by WILDFIRES. After a very dry start to 1910, for two days in August the "Great Fire" raged through the eastern parts of Washington and British Columbia and into Idaho and Montana. It was one of the largest ever forest fires in the U.S., destroying an area the size of Connecticut. There have been several serious wildfires in the PNW since then, including one in 2021, with scientists fearing that there will be even more in the future due to climate change.

The government of Canada and the Council of the Haida Nation SHARE RESPONSIBILITY for protecting this unique region and the plants and animals that call it home.

The park's name means "ISLANDS OF BEAUTY" in the X̱aayda kil dialect of the Haida language.

The waters around the islands are protected too, in line with the Haida belief that THE SEA AND THE LAND ARE ONE, with a boundary that exists only when it is drawn on a map.

Have a relaxing soak in the NATURAL HOT SPRINGS found on the island known as G̱andll K'in Gwaay.yaay.

Weathered TOTEM POLES line the beach at SG̱ang Gwaay, now a UNESCO World Heritage Site. They were carved to represent the family histories of the people who lived here. A new pole was erected in 2013 to mark 20 years of the park's shared ownership.

Learn about the islands from the HAIDA GWAII WATCHMEN, volunteers who protect cultural sites as well as guiding visitors and teaching them about Haida culture.

Gwaii Haanas National Park Reserve

If you want to explore remote rain forest landscapes and experience traditional Haida culture, then Gwaii Haanas National Park Reserve is the place to go! The traditional home of the Haida people is a land of great beauty, with forests, beaches, mountains, and fjords. The Haida Gwaii archipelago is a group of closely linked islands, and since 1988 the southern third of it has been set aside as a park and conversation area. The park has no roads, and visitors must arrive by boat or seaplane.

Gwaii Haanas is home to more than HALF A MILLION SEABIRDS, including puffins, auklets, and murrelets. Other birds, such as shearwaters and albatrosses, are seasonal visitors as they migrate.

Hike through DENSE FORESTS of ancient Sitka spruce and cedar trees. The moist climate feeds the moss that covers nearly every surface.

Keep your eyes peeled for FOREST ANIMALS such as black bears, pine martens, and ermines. In the waters around the islands you'll see dolphins and sea lions, as well as several different species of whales.

Get a better view by PADDLING A KAYAK through the waterways between islands, surrounded on all sides by incredible natural beauty.

Remains of wooden HAIDA LONGHOUSES are visible in some places, offering clues about the Haida way of life.

The park's crest shows a SEA OTTER AND A SEA URCHIN. Sea otters were once plentiful here, and they protected the kelp forests by eating the sea urchins that damaged them. Thankfully, sea otters have recently returned to the islands.

Weird, Weirder, Weirdest

The Pacific Northwest has long prided itself on being a little weird. Sometimes the really fabulous things in life don't neatly fit into any one category, but that's kind of the definition of quirky, isn't it? Here you'll find a healthy dose of random oddness, all gathered together in one place!

At the WEST COAST GIANT PUMPKIN REGATTA, racers hollow out massive vegetables, grab a paddle, and take to the water. Just like Cinderella's magic pumpkin coach ... only wetter!

At the Tillamook County Fair in Oregon, racers drive stripped-down Model T Fords (an early type of car). To add to the fun, they CARRY SQUIRMING PIGS under their arms as they zoom around the track.

At Riverfront Park in Spokane, you can visit the GARBAGE GOAT, a metal animal sculpture with a vacuum-powered mouth that sucks up trash!

Sometimes you have to race to the toilet, but have you ever raced *in* a toilet? Every January in Conconully, Washington, teams build WOODEN OUTHOUSES, mount them on skis, and race them down the street—two people pushing, one sitting on the toilet seat!

The PNW may be well-known for legends of Sasquatch—the large, hairy creature, often called Bigfoot, who is reported to roam the regions' forests. But Oregon has its very own (and even weirder!) mystery monster. Witnesses have described COLOSSAL CLAUDE as a huge, serpent-like sea monster with a horse-like head.

The town of BORING, OREGON, didn't get its name because there's nothing to do—it's named for early settler William Harrison Boring. But that didn't stop residents teaming up with two perfectly-named sister cities: Dull, Scotland and Bland, Australia!

BORING →

A tree in Washington has EATEN A BIKE! Its trunk has grown around a rusty old bike, swallowing it up and holding it 7 feet off the ground.

Tucked down an alleyway near Pike Place Market in Seattle, you can find an entire WALL OF CHEWING GUM! The wall started gathering gum in the 1990s and hasn't stopped since.

In 2007, Oregon gymnast Ivan Koveshnikov set a world record by doing 1,714 CARTWHEELS IN AN HOUR. Bet he was dizzy afterward!

A community center in Duncan, British Columbia set a Guinness World Record for having the world's LARGEST HOCKEY STICK above their entrance, at forty times life size. That made it more than 200 feet (61 meters) long!

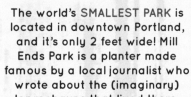
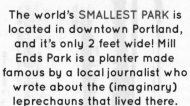

During the Second World War, an airplane factory in Washington was camouflaged by Hollywood set designers to protect it from being bombed. They built an entire FAKE SUBURB on the roof, including houses, roads, trees, and cars.

The world's SMALLEST PARK is located in downtown Portland, and it's only 2 feet wide! Mill Ends Park is a planter made famous by a local journalist who wrote about the (imaginary) leprechauns that lived there.

A hoax website about the imaginary PACIFIC NORTHWEST TREE OCTOPUS is now used to teach children not to believe everything they read on the internet!

When the only bank in North Bend, Oregon closed during the Great Depression, resourceful residents decided to make their own WOODEN COINS. The beautiful coins are now extremely collectible, and can still be used to buy things in North Bend!

Index

Major League Professional Sports Teams

National Football League/Canadian Football League
Seattle Seahawks, BC Lions
Major League Baseball
Seattle Mariners
National Basketball Association/Canadian Elite Basketball League
Portland Trail Blazers, Vancouver Bandits
Women's National Basketball Association
Seattle Storm
Major League Soccer/Canadian Premier League
Portland Timbers, Seattle Sounders, Vancouver Whitecaps, Pacific FC, Vancouver FC
National Women's Soccer League
Portland Thorns, Seattle Reign
National Hockey League
Seattle Kraken, Vancouver Canucks
Major League Rugby
Seattle Seawolves
National Lacrosse League
Vancouver Warriors